Relief from Grief

Your Relationship with God, the Key to Recovery

James E. Price

Vision
PUBLISHING
Carson, California

Relief From Grief
Your Relationship With God, the Key to Recovery
ISBN 0-9651783-5-8
Copyright © 2003 by
James E. Price

Published by:
Vision Publishing
P. O. Box 11166
Carson, California 90746-1166
1-800-478-7925

DEDICATION

A good wife crowns a man's life. For 33 years, my wife, Dolly, has been my crown, my greatest gem. I daily thank God for her and the four wonderful children we have produced — James, Michael, Robert and Connie Marie. I also thank Him for my two beautiful daughters-in-law, Erica and Norma, and for my three grandchildren, Cesar, Cesarie, and Ryan. It is to these ten that this book is dedicated.

TABLE OF CONTENTS

INTRODUCTION

For most of us, no hurt can ever compare with the loss of a loved one. It's as if a vital part of our being has been ripped away, and we're expected to continue on as usual without it. The truth is we *can* make it. Wounds heal, hurts fade away in time, life goes on and so must we. Jesus is our life, and as long as we're connected with Him we are whole and we have the strength to keep going. He always makes the pain go away. There can be a wonderful life on the other side of loss, but we must be brave enough to seek it.

Some don't have this knowledge and suffer terrible grief over the loss of companionship, the loss of a marriage, the loss of a job, the loss of health, the loss of a friendship, the loss of a home or business, the loss of a pet, and the list goes on. Though there will always be losses in this life, there will always be victory in Jesus. Pastor James E. Price has written a remarkably uplifting book that exhorts and inspires those dealing with losses of any type. It will be impossible to continue on in grief, sorrow and regret after reading these comforting — and challenging — words.

THE EDITORS

1

GOD WANTS YOU TO KNOW HIM

"Shall I hide from Abraham what I am doing?"

— Genesis 18:17

The scene was thick with sorrow and grief as I began conducting a memorial service in a well-known Los Angeles funeral parlor. The whole family of the deceased woman, though they were Christians, sobbed uncontrollably and one by one draped themselves over the casket, as if trying to call life back into the remains. Everyone — young and old — was in utter despair. As I watched the emotional scene, my heart went out to the survivors. Sure, they had lost a loved one, and sure, they were going to miss the deceased, but far more tragic to me was the extent of their grief. *Don't they know they'll see their mother again?* I asked myself. She had lived a long life, now her body was at rest.

1

Contrast this to another memorial service where the head of the house, a man whose family maintained a strong relationship with God, had died after a long illness. His widow and daughter spoke movingly — and humorously — about the husband and father who had passed on into glory.

Were there tears? Absolutely. A number of family and close friends wept softly, but it was an uplifting memorial. The man's widow was strong and dry-eyed. There was neither a tear in her eye nor a quiver in her voice. She thanked God for the years she had with the good man whose body lay in the casket. She told those who attended that Satan had not taken her husband's life, but he had made the choice to depart. He had "looked over into glory" and made the decision to vacate his tired body and be with Jesus, she said. When she finished, she had the mourners standing to their feet clapping and laughing. That was some celebration! And that's exactly what it should have been.

What was the difference in the two services? Knowledge of the Word. Both families would miss their loved one, but one understood that their loved one was with God. The other just knew that their loved one was no longer here. How different the depth of grief can be when a family is knowledgeable about the Word of God! Knowledgeable Christians don't despair or let the pangs of death overtake them. They know that the parting is only temporary. It's understandable that most people would cry and be in sorrow at such times. That's a human reaction. That loved one will be missed in many ways, but we are not to despair.

Unfortunately, scenes of despair are common at memorial services around the nation, especially where people have not been taught the Word of God. The Word brings understanding and comfort. Those who are properly taught know that when a loved one passes away knowing Jesus they can rejoice because they know where their loved one is. That loved one isn't lost. When we lose someone we don't know where they are. But we who are in Christ know where our deceased loved ones are. The Bible, in Second Corinthians 5:8, gives us this assurance:

We are confident, yes, well pleased rather to be absent from the body and to be present with the Lord.

We know their location — heaven. They are present with the Lord. But, unfortunately, the survivors have to deal with the lifeless body that the deceased left behind. That indeed can be tough. In doing so we have to remember that the loved one is *not* in that coffin. There's an element in the coffin — the flesh. There are two elements with God — the soul and the spirit.

The only reason the body had life was because of the spirit that inhabited it. That spirit is still alive and doing well, still functioning, still talking, still walking, and full of joy — only in the presence of the Lord rather than on earth with relatives and friends. And that's the assurance that the Apostle Paul gives us in First Thessalonians 4:14:

For if we believe that Jesus died and rose again, even so God will bring with Him those who sleep in Jesus.

Those who "sleep" in Jesus are going to return with Him. That's where our loved ones who had accepted Him as Lord and Savior are — with Him. They are not in the ground. They are with Him. And He's going to bring them with Him when He returns.

Paul goes on to say in Verse 15:

For this we say to you by the word of the Lord, that we who are alive and remain until the coming of the Lord will by no means precede those who are asleep.

We are all going to join Jesus when He returns. However, we who are alive will not rise to join Him before the bodies of those who have died are raised from the grave. Verse 16:

For the Lord Himself will descend from heaven with a shout, with the voice of an archangel, and with the trumpet of God. And the dead [bodies] **in Christ will rise first.**

The graves are going to open up. It may sound a little eerie, but it's going to be a great sight. Every time I do a memorial service I let people know that the separation is a temporary thing. All the graves, all the tombs, all the crypts are going to open up when Jesus comes, just as it happened when Jesus was resurrected. The Bible says the departed loved ones of many who were still alive came out of the graves and were walking through the towns. That's just a foretaste of what's going to happen when Jesus returns.

Matthew 27:52-53:

52 **and the graves were opened; and many bodies of the saints who had fallen asleep were raised;**

53 **and coming out of the graves after His resurrection, they went into the holy city and appeared to many.**

The Bible says in Ephesians 4:8 that when He went up to heaven, Jesus led *captivity* (the souls and spirits of the dead saints that were in Paradise) *captive and gave gifts unto men*. Remember, Jesus went into the heart of the earth for three days and three nights, suffering indescribable torment for us, and at the end of the three days and three nights, the heavenly Father said, *"That's enough! He has met the demands of justice!"*

Jesus hurled back the forces of darkness, snatched the keys of death and hell from Satan, and told those departed spirits of the righteous — the captives who were waiting in Paradise — *"It's time to go up!"* Since that time, every believer who departs this life before Jesus returns no longer waits in the heart of the earth, where Paradise was. He goes immediately to be in His presence in heaven. That's where Paradise has been relocated. The Apostle Paul gives us that understanding in the Second Corinthians 12:2-4:

I know a man in Christ who fourteen years ago — whether in the body I do not know, or whether out of the body I do not know, God knows — such a one was caught up to the third heaven.

And I know such a man — whether in the body or out of the body I do not know, God knows —

how he was caught up into Paradise and heard inexpressible words, which it is not lawful for a man to utter.

Paul saw things in heaven that he couldn't even tell his contemporaries at that time. Sometimes God gives us information that we can't share with others. Over in the Book of Revelation it says that seven voices uttered things to John, and when he got ready to write, they said: *"No, hold up! That's not for people today. That's for the people during the end time."* (Revelation 10:4).

We all face grief at some time in our lives, but we need to prepare for it so that when it comes we will be able to go through it victoriously and not let the enemy steam-roll our emotions. We prepare for it by meditating the Word of God and by understanding what He says about the loss of a loved one, or the loss of anything else.

Often, the worst cases of loss are the deaths of the young. Such tragedies are hard to deal with under any circumstances. Los Angeles, New York, Chicago, Atlanta, St. Louis, Detroit, San Francisco and many other urban centers bury their young too often. Teen suicides, drive-by shootings and other forms of gang killings are a constant and frightful reality in the cities. Added to those are shooting outbreaks on school campuses, accidents by drunken teen drivers, child abuse, and the deaths of young people by natural means. The young are so vulnerable. You hear of child abductions, child neglect, child abuse, children drowning in unsupervised swimming pools, and the list goes on. It's easy to see why urban undertakers are kept busy with a stream of young corpses. When old folk are burying the young, a curse is in operation. We are in a warfare and our enemy is Satan. Satan is the author of death, as Hebrews 2:14 indicates:

> **Inasmuch then as the children** [meaning people who are saved] **have partaken of flesh and blood, He Himself likewise shared in the same, that through death He might**

destroy him who had the power of death, that is, the devil.

Jesus came to destroy the works of our enemy, and that's exactly what He did. He stripped Satan of all power and authority over us.

First Thessalonians 4:13 tells us:

But I do not want you to be ignorant, brethren, concerning those who have fallen asleep, lest you sorrow as others who have no hope.

The Apostle Paul wrote — **"as others who have no hope."** He doesn't want us to sorrow as those who have no hope. If we do not know and understand the Word of God, we can sorrow, we can hurt, and we can be in excruciating emotional pain. But Paul says we should not be ignorant; we should not be uninformed concerning those who have died — or fallen asleep. We should not be ignorant concerning them, especially if they are in Jesus.

It's very important to understand the expression, **"as others who have no hope."** Outside of the Word of God people don't have much hope. They don't know what to think. Like the family sorrowing in the funeral parlor, they don't know how to deal with grief, and without the proper relief they may carry the hurts and pains of loss for years to come. There are millions of people who have gone through bad experiences as children but have never gotten relief. They carry the pains of those experiences around with them all the time, through childhood and adulthood, in and out of one relationship after another. But the Bible says that whom the Son has made free is free indeed (John 8:36). So, praise God! He has healed us from even our consciences! That's what Hebrews 9:14 tells us, and that's what we need to remember. He doesn't want us to remain in sorrow.

The devil will say to you, *"If God were real why would He let this thing happen to your loved one? You might as well forget about Christianity and salvation and all those things. You might as well go off and do what you want to do. Go get drunk, get high. Go fill yourself up with cocaine."*

He will mess with your head. He will use anything he can to get you off balance, to keep you from walking with the Lord. Some saints pray night and day for their loved ones, and when things don't happen the way they want them to happen they begin to grieve. Then the enemy comes around and asks: *"Well, why didn't God answer your prayer?"*

But most often we don't know the whole story concerning the one we've been praying for. We don't know what they believed, or where their faith was. They may have tired of this life and allowed death to come as a doorway out of their pain and struggles. We only know what *we* wanted. But if we can keep this question by father Abraham from Genesis 18:25 in mind, it may help:

"Shall not the Judge of all the earth do right?"

My answer to this question is yes: the Judge of all the earth will do right. But let's just backtrack and find out what prompted Abraham to ask that question in the first place. This was the situation: Sodom, Gomorrah and three other cities were caught up in homosexuality and other forms of sexual perversion. God had planned to execute judgment on these cities but would not do it without conferring with his friend, Abraham, whose nephew, Lot, lived in Sodom with his family. The Lord asked in Genesis 18:17:

"Shall I hide from Abraham what I am doing?"

That is relationship. God is always going to confer with those who are open to hear Him. That's the way He wants it with us. He wants to have a deep relationship with each of His children, if we'll let Him. He wants to let us know what's going on in the lives of our loved ones. He wants to let us know when they're ill or in danger. If our relationship with Him is deep enough to hear what He is saying, we can avoid many of the tragedies. He said in Revelation 3:20:

"Behold, I stand at the door and knock. If anyone hears My voice and opens the door, I will come in to him and dine with him, and he with Me."

God is saying, *"Hey, I want a relationship with you. I want us to talk. I want us to communicate."* It's one thing to accept Jesus Christ as your personal Lord and Savior, but it's another thing to develop an intimate relationship with Him. It's one thing to be married, and quite another to have a real relationship with your spouse in the marriage. The Lord wants to tell us things before they happen; He wants to help us avoid sorrow and pain. He wants to let us know where the challenges are, and prepare our hearts so we won't be jolted with the shocks of life.

God is interested in us having victory in every aspect of our lives. If we'll spend time with Him, he'll show us everything we need to know.

There's no use crying because you don't have an automobile, or a house, or a husband or wife. Spend time with Him and let Him show you how to get those things. He'll let you know what your children are getting into and what your spouse may be going through. Talk to the Father about these things. Sometimes we need to pause from other things we're doing and get some real close direction by spending time with Him. Instead, we make excuses:

"Well, what do you mean, Pastor? I'm working. I've got two jobs."

Do you have a lunch break? Then take *that* time. Do you commute to work? Take *that* time. If you're too busy to spend time with the Lord, you're too busy.

Many Christians are trying to earn enough money to build their own Taj Mahals, and they've got to work four jobs to do it. They have no time left for God. That's really not a life. The Bible says in Matthew 6:33:

> **"But seek first the kingdom of God and His righteousness, and all these things shall be added to you."**

Don't seek Him second or third. Seek Him first. He's the One who's got the answer for you.

But let's return to Sodom and Gomorrah. Genesis 18:16-23:

> **16 Then the men** [the Lord and perhaps two angels] **rose from there and looked toward Sodom, and Abraham went with them to send them on the way.**
>
> **17 And the Lord said, "Shall I hide from Abraham what I am doing,**

18 "since Abraham shall surely become a great and mighty nation, and all the nations of the earth shall be blessed in him?

19 "For I have known him, in order that he may command his children and his household after him, that they keep the way of the Lord, to do righteousness and justice, that the Lord may bring to Abraham what He has spoken to him."

20 And the Lord said, "Because the outcry against Sodom and Gomorrah is great, and because their sin is very grave,

21 "I will go down now and see whether they have done altogether according to the outcry against it that has come to Me; and if not, I will know."

22 Then the men turned away from there and went toward Sodom, but Abraham still stood before the Lord.

23 And Abraham came near and said, "Would You also destroy the righteous with the wicked?"

Here is Abraham questioning the Most High — and why not? He has a relationship with Him. The Most High tells Abraham, *"We're getting ready to destroy that place."* Abraham asks, *"Are you going to destroy the righteous with the wicked?"* That's a reasonable question. Verse 24:

"Suppose there were fifty righteous within the city; would You also destroy the place and not spare it for the fifty righteous that were in it?"

Abraham is interceding here for his nephew Lot and any other righteous people that might be in Sodom and Gomorrah. Because of his relationship with the Lord, Abraham has the right to speak up. We can get a lesson from this. Here's Almighty God, Creator of heaven and earth, listening to Abraham. Abraham wants to know how many righteous people it will take to hold back the judgment of the Almighty. Then he says in Verse 25:

"Far be it from You to do such a thing as this, to slay the righteous with the wicked, so that the righteous should be as the wicked; far be it from You! Shall not the Judge of all the earth do right?"

We need to ask ourselves this when we're facing difficulties. When we're all upset and distraught, we need to meditate on this question: *"Will not the Judge of all the earth do right?"* Right now we're breathing because He spoke air into existence. This earth is hanging in the middle of space, not crashing into anything, because He told it to *be*. The sun, moon and stars provide light because He said, *"Let there be light."* Won't the Judge of all the earth do what's right? You know He will! When you have exhausted your knowledge and understanding, ask yourself this question. Then recognize that God is still in control. Abraham knew it wasn't like the Most High to do unrighteously. He understood God's nature because he had spent time with Him.

Abraham got the Almighty to agree that He would not destroy the cities if ten righteous people could be found there. Apparently, there weren't ten righteous people there, so God got Lot and his family out, and then rained destruction on the five cities. It looked as if the only person who wasn't involved in the perversion in Sodom and Gomorrah was Lot. His wife was a little shaky, because the Lord told them to not look back when they were fleeing Sodom. But Lot's wife did look back. Apparently, she longed for what she'd left behind. The Bible says where your treasure is that's where your heart is also (Matthew 6:21). Maybe her treasure was in Sodom because she looked back and, as a consequence, turned into a pillar of salt.

We need to tell folk that God is a good God. He always tries to deliver the just. We don't know everything, and we shouldn't try to second-guess God when people we've prayed for aren't delivered, or healed, or won't act right. We don't have all the facts, but God does. It doesn't mean that He changed because things did not turn out the way we wanted them to turn out. He's the same God, and He cannot lie (Titus 1:2). The God of all the earth *will* do what's right.

Grief, however, doesn't always indicate the death. When we mention grief, it is natural to think about the loss of a loved one, but grief can affect us in other ways. Perhaps no one grieved harder than those who lost their wealth in the great stock market crash of 1929. These investors grieved so much that many took their own lives.

Others who have been seriously injured, or who have been wronged, or those who have been emotionally pained can suffer grief also. Many are grieved by divorce, the loss of a job, a wayward or runaway child, the end of a relation-

13

ship, or a debilitating sickness or disease where someone has lost all or part of their normal function. But God's Word is our answer. He gives us the victory that will cause us to overcome all hurts and pains.

Now we have a choice. We can either get into agreement with the Word or follow the leading of our feelings and emotions. We can get so distraught that we say, *"I just can't make it. Everything's terrible. The world has come to an end. I might as well just end my life."*

But first ask yourself this: Why would you end your life — the one that doesn't belong to you in the first place — if God has not given you permission to end it? You've been bought with a price, and you are not your own (First Corinthians 6:20). What are you going tell God when you meet Him face to face?

"Well, I couldn't make it down there on earth."

First, He's going to ask you, *"Who told you to take your life? Did I tell you?"*

"Well, uh, no. But it was so hard, Lord."

He'll say, *"But what did my Word say?"* And the Word will come to you immediately, and It will say:

I can do all things through Christ who strengthens me (Philippians 4:13).

"Well, Lord, I didn't know that worked, and it was so difficult down there and I just felt so weak."

"But what does My Word say?"

Finally, my brethren, be strong in the Lord and in the power of His might (Ephesians 6:10).

"Well, Lord, I didn't know where to turn."

"Didn't I tell you in My Word where to look?"

Looking unto Jesus, the author and finisher of *our* faith.... (Hebrews 12:2).

What excuse do we have?

2

UNMOVED BY THE CIRCUMSTANCES

No temptation has overtaken you except such as is common to man …

— First Corinthians 10:13

I had been battling a hypothyroid condition for more than a year. The illness made me sluggish and sleepy, and caused me to gain weight and generally have no pep. I had just become aware of some of the famous healing ministries around the nation, but at first it was as if they were simply speaking empty words. I'd see Kathryn Kuhlman and other evangelists on television, and I became curious to know whether such healings were real. I began to search the scriptures for myself. I saw how healing and salvation were inseparable. I saw where it says, **"He Himself took our infirmities and bore our sicknesses"** (Matthew 8:17) and, **who Himself bore our sins in His own body on the tree, that we, having died to**

sins, might live for righteousness — by whose stripes you were healed (First Peter 2:24). Slowly, I began to accept the Word as truth.

Finally, I prayed, *"Lord, Your Word tells me that You heal, so I'm accepting it as fact that you have provided healing for me. Based on your Word, I accept my healing and I thank you for it and give you glory and honor."*

Of course, I didn't understand everything then that I understand now. At first, I just followed what everybody else was doing. I began to confess (or declare) what the Word of God said. I went through some struggles, because the devil always attacks the mind, but eventually — praise God! — I got my healing.

It's the same with grief. We have to recognize that if there is anything hurtful, negative or depressing in our lives, Satan is going to do everything he can to reinforce it. That's the reason the Bible tells us in Second Corinthians 10:5: **casting down arguments and every high thing that exalts itself against the knowledge of God**.

When I found out that healing belonged to me, I began to declare boldly, *"Lord, I believe I receive my healing in Jesus' name. I believe that I am healed of this thyroid condition. I believe that I'm healed from the top of my head to the soles of my feet."*

"What are you doing?" the devil asked me.

I said, *"I'm confessing God's Word."*

He said, *"You don't feel any different, do you?"*

But I said, *"It doesn't matter how I feel. I'm not walking by how I feel, I'm walking by faith, based on God's Word."*

When I went to my first examination after my diagnosis, I was excited and exhilarated with the expectation of hearing good news. The doctor went through his usual checks and the technician took my blood and put me through a battery of tests.

When the results came back, they were a big letdown. *"Your condition has worsened,"* the doctor told me. That was *not* what I wanted to hear. At first I was crushed, and I asked the Lord what happened. I had gone to church, prayed, paid my tithes, read my Bible, made my confessions, and done everything the Lord told me to do. I didn't know why there was a worsening in my condition.

That's when the devil jumped in my chest.

"That didn't work for you," he said. *"It won't work for you. It doesn't work for everybody, because if it worked for everybody it would have worked for you."* So the battle raged on in my mind.

It's the same way with grief. The devil comes and brings these thoughts: *"Well, you know, you've lost your loved one, or you've lost your job, or you've lost your boyfriend (or girlfriend), so you can forget it. It's over for you."*

Typically, the devil goes to extremes. When something bad happens, he asks: *"Why don't you just kill yourself?"* He's trying to get you to do his job — on yourself. But the Holy Spirit asks, *"Who told you to stop believing just because you got some bad news? Continue to believe."*

We want to feel sorry for ourselves and get someone to sympathize with us so we can bawl and squall together. We want to have a pity party and send out invitations to our three best friends — me, myself and I. But the Spirit of God will not let us alone. He reminds us that we are not to stop believing because of what the doctor said. The doctor's report doesn't change God's Word, so we must continue to believe.

Believing and Receiving the Healing

I finally got myself together, cleared my throat and began to declare, *"I believe I have received my healing in Jesus' name, and I'm standing on the Word of God."* I was a little shaky at first, but I went on making the confessions for another three or four months between examinations. Eventually, I had it going in high gear. I was exclaiming, *"Glory to God, praise God, I know I'm going to hear a good report now."* I went back to the doctor's office and let them take some more blood with the thought that I would hear a good report. But the doctor told me, *"This is worse than it was the last time!"*

Again, that was not the news I wanted to hear. But I was a little stronger at that point and I wasn't moved as easily. I went back to look at what the Word of God said, and when I opened the Bible, it was still there: **"He Himself took our infirmities and bore our sicknesses."** The scripture didn't change, so if the scripture didn't change I wasn't going to change. I continued to confess my healing. I just said, "Okay, doctor," and went my way.

I don't argue with people who cannot agree with me, because all we've got is an argument. Amos 3:3 asks: **Can two walk together, unless they are agreed?** The answer is no. Doctors are trained to diagnose our health condition, not to debate our faith. We need to understand the difference and agree to disagree so we can move on. There's no virtue in arguing these issues.

I continued to make my stand. Another three or four months went by and I went through another examination. The third examination was still a bad report. I wasn't moved by that one either. I continued in faith. So long as I stayed in the Word I was all right. When I drifted off and started soaking up too much *Gunsmoke* and other popular television programs of the '70s, I got weak. But when I pulled away from television, got into the Word of God and started allowing the sharp, two-edged sword to cut off all the things that were not right, I began to walk in the righteousness that God has called me to, and I was strong.

When I went through the fourth examination, they said my condition was still worse. My mind was beginning to ask, *"Well, how long is it going to take?"* But my spirit rose up and said, *"I don't care how long it takes. I don't care if it's a hundred years, I don't care if it's a thousand years. I'm standing on the Word of God. If I die and go to heaven, I'll be still standing on the Word of God."*

I had to become that way; I couldn't let the devil intimidate me. He always tries to intimidate people with death. But remember this: If we die, we gain (Philippians 1:21). We don't lose. Never be afraid of death. That's nothing to be afraid of because, as believers, we'll immediately be ushered into the presence of God. That's not a bad place to be. But while we're here on earth, we should remain as long as we can so that we can get the work done and please the Father. We don't need people dying at an early age.

The Bible says *with long life will He will satisfy us and show us His salvation* (Psalm 91:16). So I said, *"No, you don't intimidate me, devil."* You get to a point where you push out that last little vestige of fear that tries to hold you hostage. I continued to take my stand and declare what God's Word said, and when I went back for my fifth examination, the doctor said, *"You know, I can't find a thing wrong with your thyroid. It's functioning wonderfully."* Don't you know I wanted to jump off that examination table and dance around that room? God's Word works! It was a stand of faith for more than 18 months, but God's Word works.

A couple of years after that a sister in Christ told me that she had been healed from the same condition in *two* months. Then the devil wanted to shoot questions into my mind about that: *"What's wrong with you? It took you 18 months to get your healing."* No, I had my healing the very first day I believed! The time matters not. That's not the issue. The issue is the fact that I believed, that I had faith and rested in His promises. I rejoice with anyone who receives from the Father God. There should be no competition in the body of Christ. I don't care if the Lord blesses another person and causes them to be prosperous while I'm still believing for my prosperity. I'm not going to get angry, upset or jealous with them. We're family. I'm happy for them. Another is riding around in his nice car while I'm taking the bus. That's all right. I love them because they're family. This is the way we all should be thinking. Our faith can get us the same thing — if that's what we want. We just have to do what God's Word tells us to do.

God has provided His Word so we can deal with any contingency, but remember, the battle takes place in the mind. The devil attacks the mind immediately. That's the reason we have to make sure that our minds are constantly exposed to the Word of God. They have to be balanced with the Word of God. The enemy wants to cause an imbalance where we're depressed and down, because grief is a doorway through which depression and almost everything else will try to come in.

The Mind — An Awesome Creation of God

The mind is a peculiar and masterful thing. It's an awesome creation of God. But if we don't have our minds

21

situated in the proper way, we're going to lose control of them to Satan, and he will do everything he can to destroy us. But God has already said: **Let this mind be in you which was also in Christ Jesus** (Philippians 2:5). We have the power to let this happen by feeding on the Word of God.

What kind of mind did Jesus have? He had the kind of mind that let Him see things the way God saw them. He went to a house where a girl was dead and said, *"She's not dead. She's just sleeping."* That's the mind of Christ. At another time when He had just finished ministering to thousands of people in the countryside, the disciples told Him, *"You need to let these people go so they can get some food. They've been with you for three days."*

(That must have been some powerful preaching! To stay with the preacher for three days and not be worried about what you're going to eat. Today, we have the biggest struggle just keeping people's attention. They're in the service looking at the clock and the minister has only been preaching for 15 minutes. They think: *"Whew! I've got a whole 45 minutes left."* They're trying to listen to the message and all of a sudden their stomachs begin to growl and ask, *"How long, how long?"* The big questions in their minds are, *"Where are we going to eat?"* and *"Did I turn off the oven when I left?"* They're fighting to stay awake. The poor pastor is preaching his heart out, and suddenly everyone hears a man on a back pew snoring loudly while a woman on the front row is losing the sleep battle as her head bobs up and down.)

The people listening to Jesus forgot their hunger and stayed with Him for three days. When His disciples told Him that He needed to let the people go and get food, He said, *"You give them something to eat."* They asked,

"What do we have? All we've got are a few loaves and some fishes. That's not enough to feed all these people." But the mind of Christ said it was enough.

We serve the God who is more than enough! He didn't retire from being the great El Shaddai. He didn't retire from being Jehovah-jireh, our broad provider. Jesus blessed the fish and the loaves and had the people sit down, and the disciples began feeding the folk until everyone was full. Then they took up the *basketfuls* that were left! That's the mind of Christ. The mind of Christ always finds a way.

He will give us wisdom, insight, direction, guidance and understanding in the hour that we need it. We're not caught unawares. The Bible says He will always lead us into all truth. If we have the mind of Christ we will know what needs to be done. The Bible says He will tell us of things come. He will give us the wisdom.

We have both divine and practical wisdom for what we need to do. Our minds are incomplete without being attached to Christ's. When our minds are attached to His, we have the victory that He wants us to have. He has an answer for everything we submit to Him. We will never go to God without getting an answer, even if we don't hear the answer the moment we ask. Many times He's been talking to us and has already given us the information we've been seeking, but our spiritual antennae are not sensitive enough to pick up the signals because of all the distractions around us. But when we get closer to Him — tuning out the distractions — we will hear His voice.

James 4:7 tells us to *submit ourselves to God, resist the devil and he will flee*. But we have to submit to God first. Then we can *resist the devil and he will flee from us*. If we try to resist the devil first without submitting ourselves to God, we'll come away whipped. We're going to be wondering, *"What's the problem?"* We must submit ourselves to God first, because in any battle, in any fight, in any warfare, we need to have a successful strategy to be victorious. Our strategy comes through our relationship with Him. In Luke 14:28-33, Jesus says:

> 28 **"For which of you, intending to build a tower, does not sit down first and count the cost, whether he has enough to finish it —**

> 29 **"lest, after he has laid the foundation, and is not able to finish, all who see it begin to mock him,**

> 30 **"saying, 'This man began to build and was not able to finish.'**

> 31 **"Or what king, going to make war against another king, does not sit down first and consider whether he is able with ten thousand to meet him who comes against him with twenty thousand?**

> 32 **"Or else, while the other is still a great way off, he sends a delegation and asks conditions of peace.**

> 33 **"So likewise, whoever of you does not forsake all that he has cannot be My disciple."**

We have to have a divine strategy. When we seek the Father God, He gives it to us. He says in Luke 11:9-10:

9 **"... ask, and it will be given to you; seek, and you will find; knock, and it will be opened to you.**

10 **For everyone who asks receives, and he who seeks finds, and to him who knocks it will be opened."**

The Lord won't come to us saying, *"Hmm, let Me see if I'm going to answer your question,"* or *"Let Me see if I'm going to open this door for you."*

No, he says to ask and we will receive, seek and we will find, knock and it shall be opened. That's a promise He's made to us. That's the reason every believer needs to understand that they're not waiting on God to do anything. The only wait is serving Him and being a doer of the Word. We're not waiting on God to see if He's going to make up His mind. He already knows what He's going to do. He knew what He was going to do before the foundation of the world. It's already set in motion. We're not waiting on God; He's waiting on us.

As believers we can't be like children. Children ask such questions as, *"When is God going to come? When is God going to answer? How long is it going to take the Lord to do this or that?"* We simply need to do what we're supposed to do in the interim. When we do our part, God has already done His part. We'll always get an answer from the Lord. He will always show us what to do in any situation. We're never left not knowing. Yes, the devil is going to try to get us over there in Wonderland with Alice, but just know that we have the victory through Jesus. We don't have to wonder what the Lord wants us to do. We have to operate in the confidence He said we have.

First John 5:14-15 says:

14 Now this is the confidence that we have in Him, that if we ask anything according to His will, He hears us.

15 And if we know that He hears us, whatever we ask, we know that we have the petitions that we have asked of Him.

I'll never forget the time when Oral Robert's daughter died in a plane crash. Oral was broken up. His wife, Evelyn, took it a lot better than He did. He could barely talk, but one thing he made perfectly clear: *"I still believe my God, and I will never, never, never reject Him."* That's the way it is. God is not our problem. Death is an enemy (First Corinthians 15:26). People who blame God are not grown up enough in the things of the Lord. That's not to put them down, but they don't know. They either have no relationship with Him, or they have a poor one.

Stopping the March of Time

As human creatures, we all want the clock to stop, especially at certain periods or seasons in our life. We want to freeze time so we can savor the moment with our loved ones. We don't want them to go anywhere. We want to talk with them on the phone; we want the security of having them near, but things are not going to last forever. Wherever we are right now is a temporary place.

Jobs provide us with a good example. We shouldn't go on jobs these days looking at them as long-term. The age of the long-term job has gone. I grew up in Saginaw, Michigan, in the '60s, ninety miles north of Detroit. All of Michigan from Bay City, to Midland, to Detroit was auto

26

town. All the cars were made in that region. There was no reason to go to school. If you could sign your name you could get a job in a foundry, and you made more money than a guy finishing his first year of college. There was no incentive to get an education. Everybody thought it would be that way forever. I thank the Lord that He led me away and I never got involved in the foundry. There were certain things that I desired to accomplish, and I knew I wasn't going to accomplish them there. My future wasn't going to be working in a foundry. God had other things for me, and I found out what they were.

Everyone thought that working in the auto industry was going to be a life-long situation. Then all of a sudden plants started closing down. They didn't need manpower because technology had taken over. The companies found that they could accomplish the same amount of production in a few plants as they could in many plants. It devastated many of the men because their pride was tied up in those jobs. It was hard for some to walk upright when there was no money coming in. All of a sudden they couldn't tell their wives to spend what they wanted or needed to spend. Here they were, trying to hold down expenses and everything in the house was breaking down.

Many of the workers never got ready for change. When the plants shut down, they were devastated. Some complained that they couldn't take care of their families. When things were rolling along, everything was good. But then things went haywire.

There were no jobs. All they heard wherever they applied was, *"You're not skilled,"* or *"You're underqualified,"* or *"You're overqualified,"* or *"You don't meet our profile."* Thousands of heads of houses lost their sense of direction. Some were depressed. Some were grieving. Some found it hard

27

to function. It's as if their bodies were in a vise and they couldn't get out. Their minds began to play tricks on them because they couldn't find solutions. If they could find solutions, they could get relief. But without solutions there was no relief, so their minds went *tilt*. Pretty soon some said, *"I'll just take this drink to relax me."* They couldn't afford Jack Daniels any more, so now it was cheap wine. Some became winos. They lost concern for themselves, and their families. Some began living on the streets. With their sense of pride gone, there was nothing left but to beg. *"Got a quarter? Got change?"*

The devil said, *"I've got you."*

Obviously, that scenario didn't happen to everyone. Some men landed on their feet economically. Some moved away. Others found jobs that didn't pay quite as well, but provided a living. Still, it happened enough that hundreds got lost in the shuffle. I don't look down on these folk, but they got that low because they didn't have the direction of the Lord. And you can't throw social programs at people and expect there to be change. You haven't dealt with the thing that got them in trouble in the first place. To make a change in the mind, there's got to be a change in the heart. Only one thing can make that change a long-lasting one, and that is the Word of God.

The Word becomes the foundation for all things. It doesn't matter that the jobs are gone, because we know that God will provide. When there is a layoff, instead of fainting, instead of going berserk and trying to figure out what we're going to do, we laugh and say, *" Glory to God, I can count it all joy!"* (James 1:2). Others are watching and saying, *"He's crazy, man. This guy has really gone off the deep end. Look at him; he's over there smiling. They ought to cart him away in a straitjacket."* But when you have knowledge of Him, then you know you have the direction, and you can say: *"Oh, you may strip me of my job, but you can't strip me of my faith. So long as I have the Word on the inside, I know God will take care of me."*

Joseph is a prime example of what can happen to a man who is guided by the Word of God. His whole family was against him. His brothers grew up in the same home, but they hated him so much that they sold him into slavery. Dealing with that kind of hatred and rejection is hard, and we know Joseph didn't say much. That's the beauty of Joseph. The only time he spoke was when God spoke to him. That's safe. When we trust in Him, He'll give us the words to say. Sometimes our minds go a hundred miles an hour and we want to say everything the way we feel it. But it's not always good to spout off with what we feel or what we think.

Several years ago, my family and I were driving back east and we went through Amarillo, Texas. This was the first time we were ever in Texas. I said, *"Honey, we're getting ready to go into the South."* The only thing I had heard was that they hanged black folk and that the police would pull you over and put you in jail.

We walked into this restaurant and this big tall dude with a loud voice came toward us as we entered the door. In my mind, when I saw him approaching, I thought, *"Oh, Lord, are we going to have to tangle?"* But he just greeted us as he exited. Inside, I got the best service I had ever had. I wanted to stay there. I got better service in Amarillo than I'd had in some places in California. In my mind I thought I was going to have a problem — but I never said it. When we say negative things we give Satan permission to cause them to happen. If we trust the Lord, He'll take us through.

29

The devil sniffs out trouble. If we're expecting trouble, it'll find us. He'll do his very best to accommodate us. If we're looking for prejudice and expecting racism, we're going to find them. That's the reason we have to put our total trust in the Father God and let Him work things out for us. If we allow ourselves to be moved by fear we'll never be victorious.

We have the responsibility to cast down imaginations. That's what Joseph had to do. He put his trust in God and God delivered him and put him where he was the most trusted slave in Potiphar's house. He had control of everything. He had so much control that his master had to find out from Joseph what he owned. He didn't know the extent of his own possessions, but Joseph did. That's trust.

Then the boss's wife got involved. She liked Joseph's leadership. She liked his strength, his assuredness. She wanted to get rid of her husband and follow Joseph. But Joseph said, *"Oh, no, no, no. I serve God. I can't do this before Him."*

A lot people would stay out of trouble if they would practice the presence of God. Wherever we go, whatever we do, the Father is already there. It would help if we could remember, *"I'm not here by myself. It's me, the Father God, the Lord Jesus, and the Holy Spirit."* Wherever we may feel alone, we're not alone. There's a full house wherever we are. There are angels about us, too.

The devil wants to blind our minds. There's an old adage that says, out of sight, out of mind.

Second Corinthians 4:4 says:

Whose minds the god of this age has blinded, who do not believe, lest the light

**of the gospel of the glory of Christ, who is
the image of God, should shine on them.**

That's why we have to write things down and put
ourselves on a schedule. It's so important to keep at the
top of our schedules prayer, praise and fellowshipping
with the Father God. We need an appointment with the
Lord everyday. We make appointments to see our clients,
our bosses, and our co-workers, so we should make daily
appointments with God. If the mind is not controlled by
the Word of God, it gets out of hand. When it's not properly controlled, it's going to get into situations that are
ungodly. We need to make sure we possess the mind of
Christ.

We need to prepare for things. We need to recognize
that we're going to have to face certain things. We can't
think things are going to continue on as they are forever,
because they're not.

3

GETTING THE
HURT OUT

"I will never leave you nor forsake you."

—Hebrews 13:5

God has not left us to our thoughts, abandoned us to our emotions, or orphaned us to our hurts and sorrows. We have not been left to drown in our depressions. We have resources. God has given us His Word to help us stand tall.

We are never alone; we are never by ourselves in grief. The devil would like to make us think that we're alone, that nobody understands how and what we're going through, but God knows and understands. That's why He says in Matthew 11:28, **"Come to Me, all you who labor and are heavy laden, and I will give you rest."** But there is a qualifier. We've got to *come* to Him. When you wrap the Word of God around you, the Holy Spirit pulls you up and lifts you out of the hole.

One definition of the word *grief* is "a deep, poignant distress caused by ... bereavement; a cause of such suffering; an unfortunate outcome: disaster."[1] *Grief* implies sorrow, an "inexpressible grief one experiences in bereavement." Besides *sorrow,* other synonyms for *grief* are anguish, woe and regret.

Grief can eat at your soul. Obsessive thoughts can bore into your mind like termites chewing through wood. Grief can ravage your immune system and devour your body. Grief and stress can cause sickness and disease such as cancer. The devil wants to keep us underneath that 300-pound boulder of grief so we can't breathe or move. He'll tug at our minds and ask, *"Why go to the Lord? Why did God let this happen? You don't feel like talking anyway? Shut those blinds, get a drink, and wallow in your hurt, discomfort, and depression. You can handle the pain yourself."* But the Lord says, *"Come to Me ... where you'll find help in the time of need."*

We've got to learn the Lord's ways. His ways are good ways. His ways are the ways of victory. His ways will cause us to overcome.

The devil says, *"You go back to bed and feel sorry for yourself."* So we cry a pool of tears and keep reliving the pain, but anything that keeps us back from God is a hindrance. It's a barrier. And the whole purpose is to keep us from the victory that we desire.

The Bible tells us in Second Corinthians 10:3-4:

3   For though we walk in the flesh, we do not war according to the flesh.

4   For the weapons of our warfare are not carnal but mighty in God for pulling down strongholds.

The weapons of our warfare are mighty through, or in, God and can pull down any stronghold of grief or depression. But if the devil can make us think that we cannot pull down a stronghold, then we'll feel handcuffed and shackled, and will not reach out for the help that's available to us.

We serve a God who works through impossibilities. All things are possible to him who believes, but we've got to take courage and say, *"Lord, I'm going to stand on — and do — what Your Word says."* The devil is going to try to fill our minds with lies, unbelief, and false ideas — anything he can get away with. But Verse 5 tells us that part of our duty is:

Casting down arguments and every high thing that exalts itself against the knowledge of God, bringing every thought into captivity to the obedience of Christ.

In grief, as in all spiritual warfare, the mind is the battlefield. The mission is to say, *"No, devil, you're not going to keep me in depression. No, devil, I refuse to allow you to keep me in sorrow. Yes, I hurt and, yes, I miss my loved one; or, yes, I'm upset about what they did to me on the job; or, yes, I'm upset about how my life has turned out, but you're not going to cause me to slow down.*

"I cast down the thought of worthlessness; I cast down the thought of failure. I cast down the thought of impossibility; I cast down the thought of losing, because I'm a winner. I am strong in the Lord and in the power of His might. I can do all things through Christ who strengthens me."

We can rise above grief and disappointment with the help of the Holy Spirit. He'll raise us to where He is — *far above all principalities, power and might.*

John 8:36 says:

**"Therefore if the Son makes you free, you
shall be free indeed."**

We can live in the freedom of Christ. When we draw
close to God, He draws close to us, and we begin to realize
that we are not alone. We must make sure the Word of God
is a part of us and let it wrap us in comfort and healing.
Our feelings may not have changed, and the tears may
still come, but we have to keep saying what God's Word
says and refuse to change. Other people will tell us, *"I
know how you feel; I know what you're going through."* We
know they mean well, but most do not know what we're
going through, but Jesus does. That's the reason we go to
Him. We know that He can comfort us. We know He can
give us the peace we need, the peace that passes all understanding that keeps our hearts and minds in Him
(Philippians 4:7). So we must stay in the Word and keep
looking to Him who is the author and finisher of our faith
(Hebrews 12:2).

Don't be like Jacob, who was tricked into believing
his favorite son, Joseph, had been killed. (Actually, Joseph's
own brothers had sold him into slavery.) Jacob refused to
be comforted in his grief.

Genesis 37:32-35:

32 **Then they sent the tunic of many colors,
and they brought it to their father and
said, "We have found this. Do you know
whether it is your son's tunic or not?"**

33 **And he recognized it and said, "It is my
son's tunic. A wild beast has devoured
him. Without doubt Joseph is torn to
pieces."**

34 **Then Jacob tore his clothes, put sack-cloth on his waist, and** *mourned for his son many days* [my emphasis here]**.**

35 **And all his sons and all his daughters arose to comfort him;** *but he refused to be comforted* [my emphasis here]**, and he said, "For I shall go down into the grave to my son in mourning." Thus his father wept for him.**

Verse 34 tells us that Jacob **"mourned for his son many days,"** even though Verse 35 tells us that his other children **"arose to comfort him."** Since he **refused to be comforted** by his children, he no doubt mourned much longer than was reasonable. Is it any wonder that after discovering years later that Joseph was still alive and after being rejoined with him in Egypt, he offered this very negative view of life in Genesis 47:8-9?

8 **Pharaoh said to Jacob, "How old are you?"**

9 **And Jacob said to Pharaoh, "The days of the years of my pilgrimage are one hundred and thirty years; few and evil have been the days of the years of my life, and they have not attained to the days of the years of the life of my fathers in the days of their pilgrimage."**

You have to wonder if Jacob would have had such a gloomy outlook if he had not spent so many days mourning his son, who as it turned out, went on to prosper mightily in Egypt. In reality, Joseph was the one who had every right to be bitter. His brothers had sold him into slavery, and the wife of his Egyptian master had lied on him and caused him to be put in prison. But the Lord was with him. He never lost faith in God.

How Long Has It Been?

Sometimes the devil tries to keep people in what I call a time trap. *"Oh, look how long you've been going through this. Look how long this has been happening to you. Look how long you've been in this situation."*

Don't buy that! Don't let the devil put you in a time trap! Second Corinthians 4:18 says:

> **while we do not look at the things which are seen, but at the things which are not seen. For the things which are seen *are* temporary** [or subject to change]**, but the things which are not seen *are* eternal.**

The troubles we may be going through are only temporary; they are not eternal. Believe me, you'll outlast them if you trust in God. We have the victory that causes us to overcome. We're through with Satan intimidating us and trying to keep us down and telling us it's not going to work. He doesn't recognize that it has already worked because Jesus did the work at Calvary. It's already done! Don't let the devil cheat you out of what belongs to you. You're the victorious, overcoming one. The agony will come, the sorrow will come, and the hurt will come, but they shouldn't be allowed to linger!

Approaching the Pit Bull

I have a pit bull named Kiley at home. When she's been hurt she doesn't want me to touch the area where

37

the pain is. I have to approach her gently. If she hurts, she will snap at me. She doesn't want to hurt more.

That's what happens to some people. When they're hurting and we get a little too close, they snap at us. It hurts to talk; it hurts to bring things out into the open. Just like anything else, when it hurts, you've got to put some ointment or salve on it to ease the pain.

It pays to talk and get things out. It doesn't do any good to keep the hurts bottled inside. We need to get help, and we get it by going to the right people. Go to those to whom the Lord directs you. Don't tell your hurts all over the place, because you need to know that people have the right motives and have your best interests at heart. Let the Lord show you to whom you should go.

Jesus came to heal the brokenhearted. I don't care how much we hurt, how much we're going through, He's able to heal us. He came just for that. Even if you're going through something right now, He came just for that. He needs you to let Him come and put the healing agent, which is His Word, on the hurt. People who love the Lord, who know God, can tell you and direct you to the places you need to go. That's what the body of Christ is all about.

In Jesus Christ, *"Whatever you go through, you grow through,"* as one of my colleagues, Pastor Milt Jackson of Las Vegas Christian Center, says. You're going to *grow* through the change, not just *go* through the change.

And you'll become stronger.

4

THE STAGES OF GRIEF

**Surely He has borne our griefs and carried
our sorrows.**

—Isaiah 53:4

I was working in my front yard one day and had Kiley
on a leash with the leash wrapped around a shovel.
Someone happened to come by and Kiley darted off,
taking the shovel with her, and causing it hit me in the
leg. Well, let me tell you, that blow had some impact!

Oddly, it didn't feel too bad at the exact moment,
but later it did. That's when the pain came. Pain always
accompanies hurt. Nobody wants to stay around pain or
hurt. We'll do almost anything to get away from them,
and that's where the enemy likes to play games with us.
He will poke at our wound, pour salt in it, and keep jab-
bing it because he wants to torture us. He'll try to get us
to quench it with alcohol, or dull it with drugs — either
prescription or illegal drugs.

Jesus identifies with us in our pain. He was beaten,
nailed to a cross, and had all of our sins placed upon

Him. We identify with Him in the fact that our sins were placed upon Him. He identifies with us in that He took our sins. Then He spent three days and three nights in the heart of the earth, being tormented. None of us knows what being tormented in hell is all about, and I'm happy to say most of us aren't going to find out. Jesus has already paid the price, so we don't have to pay it. Isaiah 53:4 is a scripture we usually use to refer to physical healing, because the word *griefs* is commonly translated to mean sicknesses and disease, and the word *sorrows* is commonly translated to mean pains. But it can quite easily refer to the pain of loss:

> **Surely He has borne our griefs and carried our sorrows.**

There is no question that Jesus bore our sicknesses, diseases, pains and afflictions on the cross, but He also bore the grief of our loss. And if He bore it, we don't have to bear it. He doesn't want us to bear the pain of grief and sorrow just as He doesn't want us to bear sickness and disease. If this is true, how can we continue in grief?

I believe the Spirit of God has shown me five stages of grief. They are *impact* and *hurt (or pain)*, which we've already mentioned, and *grieving*, *crying* and *recovery*.

Impact can occur gradually or suddenly. It might be the death of a loved one, the loss of a job, or the loss of companionship or a business deal. Usually, there is nothing in the world we can do about these losses, but try to put them behind us as quickly as possible.

Though the blood of the Lamb has redeemed us — anybody who has accepted Jesus as his personal Lord and Savior is redeemed — the enemy wants to find some kind of crack, some way to torment us. The question then becomes: are we walking in our redemption? If we're not, we're fair game for the devil.

We can be very close to God, or we might not be close to Him at all. Some have accepted Jesus, but are still drinking alcohol. Others who have accepted Him are still fornicating. Others are still taking drugs. When we have a close relationship with the Lord, such activities have to go because they cannot be in fellowship with Him. That's a decision we make, and the beauty is we have the power. We have the power to increase our fellowship with the Father God based on the time we spend with Him.

Whether it's a husband-and-wife relationship, a child-parent relationship, or a friendship, the resulting closeness is dependent on the time spent developing that relationship. It is the relationship established between the parties that will either keep us apart or draw us close.

David Didn't Let Grief Control Him

King David had stolen a man's wife, committed adultery with her, caused the man's death, and then lied about it. Nathan, the prophet of God, was sent to David. Let's look at Second Samuel 12:1-17:

1   **... And he came to him, and said to him: "There were two men in one city, one rich and the other poor.**

2   **"The rich man had exceedingly many flocks and herds.**

3   **"But the poor man had nothing, except one little ewe lamb which he had bought and nourished; and it grew up together with him and with his**

41

children. It ate of his own food and
drank from his own cup and lay in his
bosom; and it was like a daughter to
him. [I will return to this point later.]

4   "And a traveler came to the rich man,
who refused to take from his own flock
and from his own herd to prepare one
for the wayfaring man who had come
to him; but he took the poor man's
lamb and prepared it for the man who
had come to him."

5   So David's anger was greatly aroused
against the man, and he said to Nathan,
"As the Lord lives, the man who has
done this shall surely die!

6   "And he shall restore fourfold for the
lamb, because he did this thing and because he had no pity."

7   Then Nathan said to David, "You are
the man! Thus says the Lord God of
Israel: 'I anointed you king over Israel,
and I delivered you from the hand of
Saul.

8   'I gave you your master's house and
your master's wives into your keeping,
and gave you the house of Israel and
Judah. And if that had been too little, I
also would have given you much more!

9   'Why have you despised the commandment of the Lord, to do evil in His

sight? You have killed Uriah the Hittite
with the sword; you have taken his wife
to be your wife, and have killed him
with the sword of the people of
Ammon.

10 'Now therefore, the sword shall never
depart from your house, because you
have despised Me, and have taken the
wife of Uriah the Hittite to be your
wife.'

11 "Thus says the Lord: 'Behold, I will
raise up adversity against you from
your own house; and I will take your
wives before your eyes and give them
to your neighbor, and he shall lie with
your wives in the sight of this sun.

12 'For you did it secretly, but I will do
this thing before all Israel, before the
sun.' "

13 So David said to Nathan, "I have sinned
against the Lord." And Nathan said to
David, "The Lord also has put away
your sin; you shall not die."

David immediately made a 180° turn and God for-
gave him. The problem with some people is that they com-
pound the grief because they don't repent quickly enough.
When you know you've done something wrong, don't try
to excuse it or yourself. You can't beat it away, you can't
drug it away, and you can't sex it away. You've got to get
back to Him.

14 "However, because by this deed you have given great occasion to the enemies of the Lord to blaspheme, the child also who is born to you shall surely die."

15 Then Nathan departed to his house. And the Lord struck the child that Uriah's wife bore to David, and it became ill.

16 David therefore pleaded with God for the child, and David fasted and went in and lay all night on the ground.

17 So the elders of his house arose and went to him, to raise him up from the ground. But he would not, nor did he eat food with them.

David put his all into prayer for that child, just as many of us have done in praying for our loved ones. We gave it all we had at the time. But there are many cases where our loved ones, or our marriages, or our businesses died in spite of our prayers. That's when we have to recognize that we don't know everything. We don't know what agreement our loved ones had with God. Often they simply grew weary of battling the sickness or disease and decided to give up the fight. Though they told us they wanted to live, in truth they wanted to be rid of their hurting, pain-racked bodies. Believe me, it is natural to look for answers and wonder why our prayers weren't answered, but often it is because what we wanted was not what the ones we were praying for wanted. God is not going to honor our prayers over theirs. We wanted them here with us, but they wanted to go on to glory and be with Jesus. If you think about it a moment, you'll understand why someone who is very ill might make that choice. Deuteronomy 29:29 has this to say:

"The secret things belong to the Lord our God, but those things which are revealed belong to us and to our children forever...."

Usually a marriage fails because both partners are not committed equally to it, and businesses collapse for a variety of reasons, including a lack of understanding of their operation.

Still, there are some things we may never know in this life. If God wants us to know, He will tell us. Otherwise, it is best to simply leave them alone.

David lay on the ground in supplication for his child. He was the king, and kings didn't lie on the ground. He had not eaten. His servants didn't want any harm to come to him, but David would not get up. He was seeking God, and trying to change the circumstances involving his child.

Second Samuel 12:18-23:

18 **Then on the seventh day it came to pass that the child died. And the servants of David were afraid to tell him that the child was dead. For they said, "Indeed, while the child was alive, we spoke to him, and he would not heed our voice. How can we tell him that the child is dead? He may do some harm!"**

19 **When David saw that his servants were whispering, David perceived that the child was dead. Therefore David said**

to his servants, "Is the child dead?" And they said, "He is dead."

20 So David arose from the ground, washed and anointed himself, and changed his clothes; and he went into the house of the Lord and worshiped. Then he went to his own house; and when he requested, they set food before him, and he ate.

21 Then his servants said to him, "What is this that you have done? You fasted and wept for the child while he was alive, but when the child died, you arose and ate food."

22 And he said, "While the child was alive, I fasted and wept; for I said, 'Who can tell whether the Lord will be gracious to me, that the child may live?'

23 "But now he is dead; why should I fast? Can I bring him back again? I shall go to him, but he shall not return to me."

David had the right slant on grieving, which is my third stage of grief. (Remember, the first two stages were impact and hurt.) Normally, when someone we love dies, we grieve. David went through a cleansing process when he wept for the child. But after seven days, David washed himself, changed his clothes, and ate. His grieving was over. Note the difference between David's grieving and Jacob's grieving. Jacob grieved "many days."

Crying or weeping, the fourth stage, is the emotional release, but it bothers me when people tell someone who's grieving they've got to cry. Maybe some people need to, but others don't. We have to be careful that we don't try to put off our experience on someone else. Shedding a lot of tears is no indication that one loves deeply, and not shedding tears is no indication that one does *not* love deeply.

Some people cry, others don't. It's as simple as that. Everybody is different, so the responses will be different. We can't put people in a mold and expect them all to respond in the same way. We are all individuals, with different experiences. That's the uniqueness that God has built into each of us. The best way to help someone in grief is to flow with them. Be there to talk if they want to talk. Comfort them in any way you can without intruding on them. Don't expect them to act as you would necessarily. We need to find out how the Spirit of God is leading in order to assist them in the best way possible. We certainly can't dictate their emotions to them by saying, *"You've got to cry."*

Everything About Heaven Is Good

The more I realize that my loved one is in the presence of God, the more I can see the glory of heaven itself. There is nothing bad in heaven or in the presence of God, so there's really nothing to cry about. Everything I can see or find out about heaven is good. If I know my loved one has departed this life and is with Jesus, that's a good thing. The life we live on this earth is temporary anyway, but it's what we're used to, and leaving it scares some people.

A lot of people never prepare for the future; they never prepare a will, or otherwise get their houses in order, because they don't want to deal with such things. They never prepare for the eventuality of death, so they don't buy a burial policy. But dealing with those things — leaving a will, getting a burial policy — is simply good stewardship.

It's getting your business in order. It's showing concern for the loved ones who will survive you. Sometimes the fear of death keeps us from doing the things we should do. Hebrews 2:15 says:

> **...who through fear of death were all their lifetime subject to bondage.**

Fear of death causes bondage, but we should not fear death. Death is the Christian's doorway to a much better life. Those who have died are in the presence of our Lord. We will see them again, either when we ourselves die, or when Jesus returns. That's why the Bible in First Thessalonians 4:13-14 says:

> **13 But I do not want you to be ignorant, brethren, concerning those who have fallen asleep, lest you sorrow as others who have no hope.**

> **14 For if we believe that Jesus died and rose again, even so God will bring with Him those who sleep in Jesus.**

God says our loved ones are with Him and He's going to bring them with Him when he returns. That's what *recovery*, my fifth stage in grief, is all about. Your recovery is in Christ Jesus. You can't find true recovery in your head without the Word of God. You can't find true victory in the power of your mind. You've got to have substance, and that substance comes from the Word of God.

The recovery process involves doing something. What you desire is not automatically going to happen. You've got to say it. You've got to speak it. Many things will come in and try to cause you to go back into the grief and the pain, but let's remember what Paul said in First Corinthians 10:13:

> **No temptation has overtaken you except such as is common to man; but God is faithful, who will not allow you to be tempted beyond what you are able, but with the temptation will also make the way of escape, that you may able to bear it.**

As a person in Christ Jesus, there is a way to escape the pain, the hurt, and the misery, but it's our choice as to whether we take it. God loves us, and healing is in Him. That's why He said, **"Come to Me, all you who labor and are heavy laden, and I will give you rest"** (Matthew 11:28).

Let me make another point here about something that has been the cause of deep grief the world over. Remember how the prophet Nathan related the story of the poor man who lost his pet lamb to the rich man when he told David why God would punish him for the murder of Uriah? Let's revisit the verse in Second Samuel 12:3:

> **"But the poor man had nothing, except one little ewe lamb which he had bought and nourished; and it grew up together with him and with his children. It ate of his own food and drank from his own cup and lay in his bosom; and it was like a daughter to him."**

Pet owners can empathize with the poor man's grief. The loss of a pet can have the impact of the death of a family member. In fact, some pet owners view their dogs, cats, parakeets, and other pets as family members, and they grieve just as deeply when they die, run off, fly away, or get stolen. We should never underestimate such losses. Pets can be extremely devoted companions, and many owners invest a lifetime of love in them.

5

HEARING HIS VOICE

"...He will tell you things to come."

—John 16:13

In Vietnam in December 1967, as the point man for my Marine platoon, I walked into a booby trap and was literally blown up in the explosion. I sustained multiple injuries — a broken femur, two broken arms, and multiple shrapnel wounds in my arms and thighs. The only thing that saved my vital organs — and my life — was the flak jacket I was wearing. Believe me, when something like that happens, the grief can seem unbearable at times. The mind mounts up all the negative possibilities, and the devil begins to tell you that you will never walk again, or never get married. You're confronted with the worst possible scenarios. The devil says, *"You look terrible and nobody will want you. The ladies won't want you any more. You'll always be a cripple."*

But I learned an invaluable lesson. After I had been in the hospital about a week feeling really low, another soldier came in who had lost both a leg and an arm in a similar explosion. This guy was in the hospital about two weeks then he got up and went out on the town. I couldn't believe it! There I was thinking, *"Oh, woe is me,"* but this guy goes out on a weekend pass. He had his arm and his leg all bandaged up, got his crutch, and left. I said, *"Lord, have mercy. Let me stop complaining. I have not lost a leg, I have not lost an arm, but he has lost both, and he's going on."*

Another soldier who had suffered a serious burn to his leg came in. He cried day and night, *"Oh my leg, my leg! Oh my leg, my leg!"* One day I asked him, *"What's your problem?"*

"I just got through telling you," he said. *"Look at my leg!"*

I said, *"Well, do you ever intend to wear pants? Nobody is going to know anything unless you tell them. You can walk; you are alive."*

That's the first thing the Lord told me when I arrived at the hospital — I was crying, *"I look bad, Lord."*

He said, *"You don't look that bad."*

I said, *"What do you mean?"*

He said, *"You're not dead."*

I said, *"Oh."*

He said, *"Get yourself together."*

I stayed in the hospital five months and got back on my feet and haven't been down again since. Praise God!

A lot of those who have been through the Vietnam War have had a terrible time dealing with the memories of what happened. There are guys all over who came home physically, but not mentally. I, too, could be pushing a cart or living under a bridge someplace, but the Holy Spirit told me, *"Look to Jesus who is the author and finisher of your faith"* (Hebrews 12:2).

I thank God that I got hold of the Word. It kept me focused. It got me through when nothing else could, and it will get anyone else through as well if they commit to it.

When others have failed us and turned aside, we must have faith in God. So long as we have faith we please Him, and when we please God, we know that He is a rewarder of those who diligently seek Him (Hebrews 11:6).

In spite of all that we may go through, there is an answer in the Word of God. We don't have to be statistics. We can allow the power of the Holy Spirit to minister to us and bring about the kind of aid and support that we need. Then we will be in a position to help somebody else.

Those who are not in God do not have the information we have, but they need it. Believers should be so saturated with the Word that they can help others who are dealing with grief. It is their most vulnerable time, and the Lord wants us — and them — to know that His Word is the answer for their distress.

The enemy only comes for three purposes: *To steal, to kill, and to destroy.* He doesn't say, *"Well, I'm going to be over next Thursday about two o'clock and I'm going to devastate you."* He doesn't send advance warning. That's the reason the Lord says to always be ready.

The letter that Paul wrote in First Timothy 6:12 tells Timothy to fight the good fight of faith. You may purpose in your heart to live a Christian life and be devoted to God, but something immediately comes in and does its best to destroy your witness. In the midst of all this, some people get angry, shake their fist at God and say, *"Why did you let this happen to me and how come I have to go through this?"* God is not their problem.

Always understand this one thing: The Sprit of God will always work in your life if you allow Him. God leads us by His Spirit and tells us of things to come. He wants to prepare us. But the human nature in us does not always listen. Just before I hit the mortar booby trap, I sensed that there was something there, and I was trying to avoid it. It might have been God trying to warn me, but my spiritual acuity was not developed at that time and I could not locate the danger. When we spend time with Him, we get to know His voice and He tells us where to walk and where not to walk.

In a variety of ways, the Spirit of God is always trying to get hold of us. That's why we say, *"Something told me I shouldn't have done that. Something told me I shouldn't have been over there at that particular time."* But God gave us a free will, and we can make whatever choices we want.

Man Makes His Own Choices

Animals are creatures of instinct. Most of them do the same thing over and over again: Some birds fly south for the winter. Whales migrate. Bears hibernate. Man, however, can choose to do anything that he wants.

I don't know why anybody would choose to live in Alaska, but they do. Why would anybody want to go to the North Pole? Who knows? The ice and the frigid climate fascinate some people. Folk look at California and say, *"No, I wouldn't be in that earthquake state,"* but they live in Oklahoma and Kentucky and other places where they have tornadoes or floods. Florida has its hurricanes. In the North and Northeast, there are snowstorms. When the snow thaws, floods come. Some people continue to live in known flood areas. Even after they have lost their homes to floodwaters, they go back and rebuild in the same place. That's free will. They know the area is dangerous and the risks are high, but it's a choice they make. There are others who spend millions to build houses on hills that may eventually give way as the earth begins to move under them. That's free will.

Following the Divine Assignment

One of the things I love is flying. I love being around aircraft. If I were not in ministry, I would probably be an airline pilot. I would enjoy that, but it's not my divine assignment. It's not what I've been called to do. You can love or enjoy something, but you've got to follow your divine assignment to please God. Still, I have a free will. I can accept my divine assignment, or do what I want to do. I choose to accept my assignment, and fly when I have the opportunity. A lot of folk choose not to follow their divine assignments, even though the Bible says the gifts and calling of God are irrevocable (Romans 11:29). In other words, once God has given you a gift, or called you to an assignment, He doesn't retract it.

At one time I thought the Lord wanted me to live and minister in Hawaii. I just knew that was the place where I should be. I told the Father while I was there, *"Father God, I'm already here. It would be a good idea for me to stay right here in Hawaii."* I had always been fascinated with the tropics. Preachers in the tropics wear short pants and short-sleeved shirts. It would have been great for me, I thought, but that was not my divine assignment. I had to obey God. There is a reward in obedience. Isaiah 1:19 says:

"If you are willing and obedient, you shall eat the good of the land."

The reason people sometimes don't eat the good of the land is because they have not gotten the two parts — willing *and* obedient — working together at the same time. Either they are obedient but are not willing, or they are willing but not obedient. Both are not working together.

55

The scripture says, **"If you are willing *and* obedient, you shall eat the good of the land."**

We are Christians on assignment. We represent the Godhead. We represent the Father God. We represent the Lord Jesus Christ. We represent the power of the Holy Spirit. God is counting on us. He has not entrusted this ministry to the angels, but to man, who is made in the image and likeness of God. We each have an assignment. That's why we should be faithful to being where we are supposed to be. If you are supposed to be a member of a particular church, be obedient to that.

The Bible says we have been bought with a price and we are not our own. We belong to the Lord (First Corinthians 6:20). But we have a powerful sense of freedom that dictates to us that we can do what we want to do when we want to and how we want to do it. God does not come down with a sledgehammer and hit us over the head and say, *"Okay, act right, now."* He's not like that. That's the reason the Bible says, **Whoever desires, let him take the water of life freely** (Revelation 22:17). God wants us to be obedient of our own free will. He doesn't want us to feel forced to love Him. That's not love.

God has wonderful things planned for us. But we get too caught up in today, looking at how big our problems are and what we have to go through. He never told us to look to our problems. He said look to Jesus (Hebrews 12:2).

So you got fired from your job, but why run around crying about it? I thought you were in Jesus. I thought He was your Savior and your Lord. If He got you the job in the first place, can't He find you another one? That's not the only job available. Somebody out there is looking for you, and probably couldn't find you because you were still working on the job you just lost. God's got a plan for you if you will submit to Him; but you've got to submit to Him.

Joseph told his brothers about his dream and they threw him into a well and sold him into slavery. Can you imagine that? But I can't find anywhere where Joseph ever complained. Joseph ran Potiphar's house, and Mrs. Potiphar was on the side watching, saying, "*He looks soooo good!*" She wanted Joseph. Nobody had ever said no to her, but Joseph did. Then Mrs. Potiphar falsely accused Joseph and he wound up in prison. Can you imagine being in prison eleven years for something you didn't do, and not complaining? Joseph found favor in prison and the officers began giving him authority. Wherever he went they would just let him take control. Listen, promotion comes from the Lord (Psalm 75:6-7).

Joseph survived his brothers' treachery, the false accusations by Potiphar's wife, the prison term, and still rose to the top (Genesis 45:8). That's the reason why, when we face opposition, we ought to say, "*Praise the Lord! Glory to God!*" Why? Because the Bible says to count it all joy when you fall into various temptations, trials and tests (James 1:2).

How can we count it all joy? Because we know that God's got a plan and He's going to work His plan in our lives if we'll allow Him, and everything will be all right. If we let the enemy come in and mess up our minds and get us distracted to the point where we're not paying attention to the Word, we're going to be caught up in confusion. God is not the author of confusion (First Corinthians 14:33), so guess who is? We can be saved, having accepted Christ as our personal Lord and Savior, and still listen to the devil. That's the reason we've got to stay in the Word.

Relief From Grief

We're going to go through some losses. Loved ones
will pass away, businesses will fail, and relationships will
fall apart. We will go through a variety of emotional
changes, but the Word is going to help us through those
times. I'll repeat what Pastor Jackson of Las Vegas Christian Center likes to say: *"Whatever you go through, you
grow through."* We're always going to go through a growing process. We learn and we become better and we go
forward.

Understand that setbacks, disappointments, failures
are only steppingstones to victory. How many failures have
most successful people had, only to eventually bring about
a tremendous victory? They refused to accept disappointment and just kept right on going, and then began piling
up successes.

It doesn't help to wallow in past mistakes or missed
opportunities. We don't need to play the lottery to hit the
big one. We hit the big one when we accepted Jesus. All
we have to do is move into the arena where He wants us to
be so we can get blessed. The Lord will supply all our
need according to His riches in glory by Christ Jesus
(Philippians 4:19). The Bible says He is able to make all
grace abound toward us (Second Corinthians 9:8).

If you're thinking you don't have anything, praise
God anyway. He gives seed to the sower, bread for the
eating, multiplies our seeds sown, and increases the fruits
of our righteousness (Second Corinthians 9:10). But we
are the ones who have to make the decision. We are the
one who have to decide that we're going to have what
God says we have.

Can you imagine the widow woman in the book of
Second Kings, Chapter 4, who was in deep poverty and
was about to lose her two sons as slaves to her creditors?

58

This woman was hurting and in grief, but she still had a choice. She could listen to the devil or she could listen to the man of God, Elisha.

The prophet asked the woman, *"What do you have?"* She said, *"I don't have anything but a little jar of oil."* (You've always got something.) He told her to *"Go borrow some vessels, and borrow not a few."* After she had borrowed the vessels she was to return to her house, shut the door behind her, and she and her sons fill the vessels with the oil. The woman had to borrow the vessels because she didn't have money to buy them, but she had favor with people and they loaned her what she needed. When she had completed her assignment, she went back to the man of God.

She didn't all of a sudden get a brainstorm and say, *"I know what to do with this."* She was very careful to only do what the prophet told her and no more. That's where a lot of people miss it. They get a little bit of what God's Word says and run with it, saying, *"I got it! I got my answer from God!"* Often the Lord is saying, *"Wait, I have more to give you! That's not all of the message!"* God wants us to learn to how listen to everything He has to share with us.

Elisha told her, *"I want you to sell all the vessels of oil, pay your debt and live on the rest."* Now here's the beauty of it. She had to pay whatever debt her husband left — including the mortgage and all the credit cards — then she had to pay the people for all the vessels she used. The prophet told her to *"live on the rest."* I love that part — not barely get along, not just exist, but *live* on the rest.

She didn't have a lot of time to stay in grief. She had to save her boys and her home. That's a lot of pressure at one time, but she went to the Lord. We must go to Him immediately when we are in trouble, or hurting, or in pain.

There is no time to find fault. Finding fault will not help us. It keeps us all broken up on the inside. It's time to get to the Father God.

Layoffs and Downsizing

The corporate world constantly goes through a lot of layoffs and downsizing. We hear in the news that this company is laying off 15,000, or another company is laying off 5,000. Almost every other week we hear of someone we know who is being laid off. That's a gut-wrenching thing, especially if you're 50-something years old, nearing retirement and suddenly find yourself without a job.

You want to know how you're going to pay your bills. When you get a certain age, discrimination starts to become a factor. You're too old, or your health is a liability, or they don't want to pay you what you're worth. Or maybe it seems that only a certain gender or certain groups are being hired. That can get you bitter quickly, but why let it? See it as an opportunity. If you are a believer with a good relationship with the Father God, you know He's got something good for you, so now you are freed to do that. Don't worry about the money. I understand that money is a major part of how things are run, but it isn't *the* major thing. The Bible says, **"But seek first the kingdom of God and His righteousness, and all these things will be added to you"** (Matthew 6:33). I happen to believe that.

The enemy wants to keep us distracted, looking at what we *don't* have instead of looking to the Father God, praising Him and saying, *"Lord God, thank You for the salvation you have given me. Thank You for letting Your Son Jesus die at Calvary's cross for my sins. Thank You, Lord, that You are the God who is more than enough. You are the God who is the great provider. And, Lord, they may have laid me off the job, they may have turned me out, and I may just be a couple of weeks from retirement but, Father, I know You've got a plan for me that will work abundantly above all that I can even ask or think. You've got a good plan for me and I accept that plan, Father God. Thank You for showing me, leading me, directing me, and guiding me in the way that You want me to go."*

Then put the devil on notice, *"Devil you're a crazy fool. I know you were behind this thing in the first place. And I rebuke you in Jesus' name. But I want to let you know that you have lost again because I'm not going out of my mind and I'm not going to lose out. My Father is going to provide for me better than when I was on the job."*

The Bible says that if we will speak to the mountain and say, *"be cast into the sea, and do not doubt in our hearts, but believe those things we say will come to pass, we will have whatever we say"* (Mark 11:23). Plus as believers, we're to call those things that are not as though they are (Romans 4:17).

How can we lose? We serve the God in heaven, the one who created the heavens and earth. He didn't make any mistakes. The God we serve is still operating in our lives. All things are upheld by the word of His power (Hebrews 1:3). Think about it. Our Daddy owns everything! If our vision is small and we're looking at our own little arena of life and that's all we can see, we can't see the bigness of God. The Father God is bigger than anything we will ever have to deal with in life. He's bigger than any challenge, any difficulty, any sadness, or any sorrow. Why in the world would we settle for less?

A lot of times we don't look to God quickly enough. Sometimes we wait until we're at rock bottom. But we have to maintain an unwavering trust in the Lord, no matter

61

what. God is never wrong. He'll never lead us astray. But if we will take the time to spend with Him, oh, what an experience! Whatever we face in life, we face it in victory when we remain in Him.

6

THE POWER OF LOVE

"For God so loved the world that He gave
His only begotten Son, that whoever believes in Him should not perish but have
everlasting life."

—John 3:16

I have given you my experience of being in an explosion as a Marine in Vietnam. I've replayed that explosion in my mind I don't know how many times. The
mind never forgets things like that: what happened, when
it happened — the whole thing. I'd be asleep or sitting
around somewhere, then — boom! I could see myself
crumpled on the ground and going through all the pain
again. I didn't know then what I know now, but something said to me during those nightmarish times, *"Hey,
let's think on something else!"*

I stopped being so concerned about myself and
started getting concerned about helping others. I got on
with my life. It was time to move forward, to get my education. So I went — arm casts and all — to school. I'd be
in school hurting, but I went anyway. Then I got involved

in the church and started doing whatever I could to help out. I was hurting, but I went on. I couldn't be worried about how bad I looked and how terrible I felt, but every once in a while I'd come into contact with someone who wanted to talk negatively. *"Oh what a terrible time you had,"* they'd say. I knew I had a terrible time, but I didn't want to dwell on that. It was a new day, a new hour, a new time. People wanted to get into debates about the war. *"Well, that was the wrong war and you guys shouldn't have been there."* Thank God for the Holy Spirit. He helped me ignore all of them.

When we continue to look to the Word of God we don't have time to feel sorry for ourselves. I did not let the injuries stop me because I kept my focus on Him. But every once in a while I'd be sitting around looking at my scars, or I'd feel the pain and the discomfort and my mind would think, *"Oh, woe is me. Oh, I was in a terrible situation. Oh, what I went through!"* Then I would shake myself and say, *"Wait a minute. Hold it. Stop! You're not supposed to be doing that."*

War does not play well on the mind. I understood how some of my fellow veterans couldn't get the horrors of Vietnam out of their heads. You need healing for your mind. You need healing for your memory. I'm here to let you know that the name of Jesus is the name you can call on and find help and healing and deliverance.

We'd been trained for combat, but people at home had a tendency to pick on us. Then we had to use self-control so we wouldn't destroy the folk in our own city. We had to remind ourselves that they were not the enemy. I used to have a terrible temper, but the love of God is greater than anything. Jesus taught me how to love folk. People are precious and valuable to Him. I don't care how bad they are, God loves them.

Tension at a Memorial Service

Once, while I was doing a memorial service, a very rough, intimidating-looking guy sitting on the front row got up during the invitation and said, *"Stop, Stop, that's enough!"* Then he turned and walked out with two rough-looking men following him. The place got very quiet. For a moment I was in disbelief and shock. But the Spirit of God said, *"Continue with the invitation and love that person."*

The atmosphere had turned cool, but I went on to give the invitation. I remembered what God said about demonstrating love, so when we got to the cemetery, I went up to the man and said, *"I'm sorry if there was anything I said that upset you."* He broke down in tears and said, *"I'm sorry, I didn't mean to cause a problem. I just couldn't take it no more."* The guy had lost a loved one and was quite distraught and emotional. I later found out that he was involved with one of the notorious gangs, and some were there at the memorial to support him. But it was the conviction of the Holy Spirit during the invitation that got to him. Rather than yield to it in front of his friends, he ran. Though he didn't receive Jesus at that time, I believe he was ministered to by the love and concern that was shown him.

We're out to win folk, not destroy them. That's what the Lord had to get over to me in that situation, as well as when I returned from Vietnam. Healing had to come to my emotions so anger and hatred wouldn't overtake me. If we start loving people, anger and hatred have no place to take hold.

I can understand that people will get angry. Some people will make you angry, but we can't stay that way. The scripture says, don't let the sun go down on your wrath (Ephesians 4:26). Don't let hatred in. God has a better way of doing things. There are good Christian folk in jail because they allowed anger and hatred to get the best of them. It isn't worth it. Follow God's way. Follow God's love. Find a new way. Get a plan from the Lord.

Again, I like how Luke 14:28-30 explains that we've got to have a plan.

> **"For which of you, intending to build a tower, does not sit down first and count the cost, whether he has enough to finish it—**

> **"lest, after he has laid the foundation, and is not able to finish, all who see it begin to mock him,**

> **"saying, 'This man began to build and was not able to finish.' "**

If you're upset about something, let God show you how to work it out. Let Him show you how to get yourself redeemed. We have to realize that He knew about the whole thing before we did. He has a plan that will help us. All we have to do is follow Him. The Bible says, **For as many as are led by the Spirit of God, these are sons of God** (Romans 8:14). If you follow that, you will come right out of whatever is troubling you. You will go on to recovery, peace and victory.

We can't sit around and hope something will happen. We're not going to get what we need watching *The Edge of Night, All My Children* or *General Hospital*. We can't watch soap operas and gain the inspiration for the real-life things we have to deal with.

66

I was listening to some of my relatives talk one day and was getting a little concerned. They mentioned some guy slapping a woman, and I asked who it was. I thought they were talking about someone I knew, but they were talking about a character in a soap opera! (Some people get so wrapped up in soap operas that they act as if they are real life.)

Take the Focus Off Yourself

Most of the time when the Lord deals with me He is getting me out of selfishness and anger and getting me over into love. When I stop thinking about myself so much, I start looking at what God's plan is all about.

We have no business hating anyone for any reason. We're believers. We're Christians. I don't care if the other person is ignorant and doesn't know what they're doing. That doesn't give us license to hate them. If you're going to do something or take some kind of action, make sure it's a wise action and not something you're doing because you're angry or upset. You only take action where you can operate from a sound mind, where you can use good judgment.

In bereavement, we usually hurt to the degree of love that we had for the deceased. But sometimes we invest so much in a person — everything, in some cases — that we need to make corrections. Remember how Jacob grieved for Joseph? God can understand that we loved mama, auntie, grandma, a husband, a wife, a child, or a job, but the Bible tells us that we are to love the Lord our God with all our heart and with all our soul and with all our mind, which is the first and great commandment (Matthew 22:37-38).

67

God is not trying to detract from the love we have for someone or some thing. He is merely trying to get our priorities straight. The love we invest in God causes us to operate in victory, and that victory will help us to handle the losses. If you want to get a good teaching on love, read and study the Book of First John. John is the apostle who also wrote the Gospel of John and Second and Third John.

First John 4:17 says:

Love has been perfected among us in this: that we may have boldness in the day of judgment; because as He is, so are we in this world.

If we want to find out how we're doing, then we must find out how Jesus is doing. If Jesus is doing all right, then we're doing all right. As He is, so are we in this world. Is Jesus victorious or is He defeated? If He is victorious, then we are victorious. If Jesus is an overcomer, then we are overcomers. Verse 18 says:

There is no fear in love; but perfect love casts out fear, because fear involves torment. But he who fears has not been made perfect in love.

What kind of love is he talking about? He's talking about the God kind of love — *agape*, or unconditional love. This is the kind of love that says in John 3:16 that **God so loved the world that He gave….** That's a powerful kind of love. God loved us when we were unlovable. We were dead in our sins and had a one-way ticket to hell and God still loved us so much that He gave His son as a sacrifice for us.

68

The Power of Love

God expects us to love so much that we give of ourselves. It is important for us to have a desire that souls be
saved. That's the reason we have a mandate to go into all
the world and preach the gospel (Mark 16:15). How are
they going to hear the message unless somebody goes?
We keep saying, *"Well, send somebody else, Lord. I'm kind of
occupied right now."* But Isaiah said, **"Here am I! Send
me"** (Isaiah 6:8). That's what we need to say.

God loves us. With that love He supplies us with all
the resources of heaven for whatever we need. Whatever
we need heaven wants to supply. The only thing that is
required is that we come in faith because without faith we
cannot please God (Hebrews 11:6).

You know it's a lie when the devil says, *"God is not
going to accept you anymore. God is not going to love you anymore."* Think about it. If God could love you before you
were saved, in all of your ignorance and sin, it's certainly
less of a problem to love you after you are saved. He didn't
like the sin you were in or your bad actions, but he loved
you. Now that you are saved and filled with His Holy Spirit,
how much more are you lovable?

Jesus said to the Father, let the world know that you
love them as you love Me (John 17:23). So when the devil
tries to put idiotic thoughts in your mind, attack them
with the Word. Tell him to shut up! Any time you believe
God for anything, always know that the devil is going to
contest every inch of ground. He's not going to sit back
and let you have it. He'll try to steal from you. He'll say,
*"You ain't never going to get over your grief. God is not going to
provide finances for you. Nobody wants you. You'll never be
healed. Prosperity is for somebody else, it's not for you."* Don't
you know that's a lie?

69

Remember, the Bible tells us that God is able to make all grace abound toward us (Second Corinthians 9:8). But we have to live right, according to the Word. We can't be caught up in self-deception. Just follow the script, which is the Word of God, and victory will come.

We've got to replace what the devil tries to program into our minds with the Word of God. We have to throw out everything that is not in line with the Word of God. We cannot remain in depression. Depression is the result of many things, from past actions to chemical imbalance. But even if it is a chemical imbalance, focus on the Word. If we keep our focus on the Word, it will help the chemical imbalance too. On the other hand, it's not wrong to go to health professionals. It's not wrong to get a checkup. It's not against our faith to do that — but in conjunction with the Word. Victory belongs to us.

Through the Lord we can go on. Through the Lord we can prosper. Through the Lord we can be successful. I understand that sometimes we get to the point where we want to set all our plans a certain way and when things don't work out, then all of a sudden we think all our plans are dead. Why? Who said the plans were dead? Why should we let go of the vision God has given us?

If you let yourself focus on the problem or condition, it will keep you down. But if you will focus on Jesus and the Word of God, it will cause you to triumph and be victorious in every circumstance.

Yes, I know you loved your loved one very much. But, if they knew Jesus, they're in a good place. You may be in hurt, but they are not. You may cry every now and then, but they are not crying. They're in a more wonderful place than you could ever imagine. They are in the very presence of the Lord. He wipes away all tears — there are no tears of sadness in heaven.

So what happens to you? You may feel lonely, left at home by yourself, but you are not alone because He is with you. He says, *"I will never leave you nor forsake you."*

I ministered to a lady once who told me she just couldn't stand to be alone, so she began "shacking up," as they say, or living with a man to whom she was not married. I asked her why in the world would she play into the devil's hands? *"Let me ask you,"* I said, *"do you feel better now?"*

"No," she said, *"What shall I do?"*

"Get out of it," I said.

You're not going to get any victory being in sin. Get out of the sin and go on to victory. God wants you to have the victory so that you might be able to stand according to His Word.

Or maybe you had a bad business deal. You got hooked up with the wrong people, got ripped off and you said you would never get involved in that business ever again. But nothing may have been wrong with the business concept; it was the people you got involved with. You may be hurt, but why would you let the devil steal your vision? Don't you realize that in Christ Jesus you have been redeemed? Don't you realize that it's not over just because you have been dealt a sore blow? Don't you understand that He has the final word? Don't you recognize that God can get the victory for you in any circumstance and situation? It wouldn't matter if you lost a fortune. Don't you know He can get it back for you?

I know folk who have been foreclosed on, lost their home, and fell apart, crying, *"Oh God, I lost my house!"*

Are they still building houses?

"You don't understand, I don't even have a job now."

Weren't you looking for one when you found that one? You mean to tell me God Almighty, the Creator of heaven and earth and the whole universe, cannot get you another job? If you listen to the Lord, He'll not only get you a job, but He'll put you into a thriving business.

Sometimes people get all stressed out over their business, but they simply need to spend time with the Father. They need to get involved with Him to find out what to do. Most of the time it's because they are not putting first things first. They get so busy that they don't have time for the Lord. They don't have time to get before Him and find out what He wants them to do.

These are simple things, but sometimes it is difficult to get on track only because the enemy has you so caught up. You say, *"Well, I'm not making enough money and I need to find out what I'm going to do about this…."*

Stop. Just cool it for a moment. You're in what I call a stall. Get on your knees before the Father God and say, *"Father, I need to get some priorities straight right now!"*

One thing I learned from flying is that any aircraft can stall at almost any time. You've got to know how to recover from it. You get the aircraft flying again by getting back to the first principles. The first thing you do is shut your engine off. (You don't really shut it all off, but you shut it down.) You fly free where you've got lift going under the aircraft, and once you've got lift, then you turn the engine back on. Then the aircraft begins to fly. It works every time.

You've got to put first things first. You've got to get straight with God. Let me tell you something: It doesn't take anymore than ten seconds to change. It doesn't take four or five weeks. First of all, change your mind. Change your attitude toward Him. Spend time with Him. Once you do that, He will start giving you the direction and guidance and show you how to gain the victory.

7

FINISHING THE COURSE WITH JOY

Weeping may endure for a night, but joy comes in the morning.

— Psalm 30:5

I like the book (and tapes) by Jerry Savelle titled, *If Satan Can't Steal Your Joy ... He Can't Keep Your Goods*. Why is that true? Because the joy of the Lord is your strength (Nehemiah 8:10). The book reads:

> As long as you have the Word in your heart, you will have joy in your heart. Then no matter what the devil does, he can't totally defeat you....[2]

> Always remember this: Satan may come against you, but he can't defeat you unless you let him. He may try to take your car, your finances, or the life of a loved one. But until he gets your joy, he can't defeat you. As long as you're still praising God and still have a joyful heart, the game isn't over.[3]

Those who have gone on before us love us, but we are not weighing heavily on their minds while they're in the presence of God. Believe me, they are not in heaven fretting over us. They have unspeakable joy. They know we'll be all right as long as we stick with the Word. So don't feel sad about them. We ought to be glad because they are in the presence of the Lord.

We here on the earth are the ones who need help. This is enemy-held territory and as believers we have to take control of it. We are constantly dealing with satanic forces. The Book of Matthew says the gates of hell shall not prevail against the church, and First Corinthians, Chapter 15, tells us that death is an enemy that will finally be destroyed. In fact, it says in verses 25-26:

> **For He** [Jesus] **must reign till He has put all enemies under His feet.**
>
> **The last enemy** *that* **will be destroyed** *is* **death.**

If God says the gates of hell shall not prevail against the church, it should be clear that God and the church stand against hell and its gates. God doesn't want to see anyone go to hell — especially our unsaved loved ones. If God says death is an enemy, it should be clear that He would not use His enemy, death, to steal our loved ones from us. Death is a byproduct of sin, which Adam allowed into the earth when he transgressed in the garden. Death will remain in force until Jesus puts all enemies under His feet, and then it too will be subdued.

Hebrews 2:14 tells us that Jesus shared in our flesh-and-blood physical likeness, as well as our human death.

In doing so, His purpose was to defeat Satan and show us how to live victoriously:

Inasmuch then as the children have partaken of flesh and blood, He Himself [that is, Jesus] **likewise shared in the same, that through death He Might destroy him who had the power of death, that is, the devil.**

Satan is the one who causes death, but for generations people have blamed God for taking their loved ones. There is no death in God, so he can't give death to anyone. But because of Adam's sin, which allowed death to enter the world, we are all headed for physical death (Romans 5:12). The only way we can avoid it is to be alive when Jesus returns, but no one knows the day or the hour of His return. Thank God, Jesus defeated physical death when He rose from the dead. Death couldn't hold Him, and it can't hold us either. For the Christian, death is merely a doorway by which we leave this world and enter into the next. That next world is everlasting life in the presence of Almighty God. That's the reason believers should never fear death.

There are times when we are spiritually and emotionally fragile, but we must make every effort to maintain our joy. Habakkuk 3:17-18 says:

17 **Though the fig tree may not blossom, nor fruit be on the vines; though the labor of the olive may fail, and the fields yield no food; though the flock may be cut off from the fold, and there be no herd in the stalls —**

18 **Yet I will rejoice in the Lord, I will joy in the God of my salvation.**

75

Remember, we always have our heavenly Father's shoulder to lean on. He is our answer. We can always find joy in Him. He sent Jesus, Who is our life. Jesus said in John 14:6:

"I am the way, the truth, and the life. No one comes to the Father except through Me."

If Jesus is the Way, then we need to follow Him, and no one else. Everyone else who tries to lead away the flock is a thief. That's why He said in John 10:10:

"The thief does not come except to steal, and to kill, and to destroy. I have come that they may have life, and that they may have it more abundantly."

The Lord leads us by His Spirit. Romans 8:14 gives us this assurance:

For as many as are led by the Spirit of God, these are the sons of God.

Being led is a two-part thing. A person can be led, but the one being led must follow. Notice, it didn't say, "for as many as are *pushed* by the Spirit of God," or "for as many as are *dragged* by the Spirit of God" are the sons of God. No, it says "for as many as are *led* by the Spirit of God." That means we have to follow. It also means our *wills* are being activated. Our wills are our choices — the same wills that we came to Jesus with.

The Father is always trying to lead us away from danger. When Moses and the children of Israel faced the Red Sea with Pharaoh's army closing in behind them, God parted the sea and led them across on dry land. When the

Egyptians tried to follow, He let the waters crash down on them. God always wants to protect His people, but their wills are involved. Consider this: Even if the enemy takes you out, you know where you are going. You end up in a better place. No believer wants to die, but none should ever be afraid of death or of dying. We've got it made either way.

Remember the widow woman whose children were about to be sold into slavery? The prophet asked her, *"What do you have?"* She said, *"I don't have anything but a cruse of oil."* God used that oil as a resource to bless her. What we have as believers are all the resources that heaven has to offer. First and foremost we have Jesus. What a comforting reality it is to know that we have the Savior!

What do you have to be concerned about when you have Jesus, the Father God, the Holy Spirit, the Word of God, and the angels of heaven? Oh, you may be hurt for the moment, but in Jesus you don't have to stay in hurt, or grief, or concern, or worry. You have joy. Look at these words from Job 8:21:

He will yet fill your mouth with laughing, and your lips with rejoicing.

My Bible tells me, **For whatever is born of God overcomes the world** (First John 5:4). It tells me that my faith is the victory that overcomes the world, and the one who overcomes is he who believes that Jesus is the Son of God.

If you believe in Jesus, then you are the one the scripture is talking about. Stamped on the forehead of your spirit is the word OVERCOMER. Every Christian has that word branded on his spiritual forehead. You may not be able to see it while shaving or putting on makeup, but it's there. Even when you don't feel like an overcomer, it's there.

It's like the tattoos that some people get on their bodies. Regardless of what day it is, that tattoo is there. Good or bad, the tattoo is there. Well, the tattoo of the spirit doesn't leave just because your feelings change. The circumstances never change God. He is always the same. He says, *"I change not."* He is the same yesterday, today and forever (Hebrews 13:8).

God is saying to each one of us, *"Come on up higher, come up to the throne of God."* He wants you to come to a higher place in Him. If we are not satisfied where we are, well, neither is God. He is willing to raise us to a higher level, or let us stay where we want to be. If you are satisfied where you are, fine. But don't fume and fuss about how bad you were treated in life. You are connected with the best resource you could ever find. How do you get up higher, closer to the throne? It's through that intimacy that He so desires to have with you — meditating His word, spending time in prayer, worship and praise. That's when you come to know Him. Psalm 91:1-16 tells us:

1 **He who dwells in the secret place of the Most High shall abide under the shadow of the Almighty.**

2 **I will say of the Lord, "*He is* my refuge and my fortress; My God, in Him I will trust."**

3 **Surely He shall deliver you from the snare of the fowler and from the perilous pestilence.**

4 **He shall cover you with His feathers, and under His wings you shall take**

refuge; His truth *shall* be *your* shield and buckler.

5 You shall not be afraid of the terror by night, *nor* of the arrow *that* flies by day,

6 *Nor* of the pestilence *that* walks in darkness, *nor* of the destruction *that* lays waste at noonday.

7 A thousand may fall at your side, and ten thousand at your right hand; *but* it shall not come near you.

8 Only with your eyes shall you look, and see the reward of the wicked.

9 Because you have made the Lord, *who is* my refuge, *even* the Most High, your dwelling place,

10 No evil shall befall you, nor shall any plague come near your dwelling;

11 For He shall give His angels charge over you, to keep you in all your ways.

12 In *their* hands they shall bear you up, lest you dash your foot against a stone.

13 You shall tread upon the lion and the cobra, the young lion and the serpent you shall trample underfoot.

14 "Because he has set his love upon Me, therefore I will deliver him; I will set him on high, because he has known My name.

**15 He shall call upon Me, and I will an-
swer him; I *will be* with him in trouble;
I will deliver him and honor him.**

**16 With long life I will satisfy him, and
show him My salvation."**

You can recover; you must recover, and go on to the
next level. Giving up is not an option; defeat is not an
option. In warfare, soldiers are taught that some of their
buddies will likely be lost, but the battle continues. You go
to combat with guys you've come to know, but you realize
they may not be around the next day or even the next
moment. Still, you have a mission to fulfill, and you must
fulfill it. You must hold your ground. If everyone gets
wiped out and you are the only one left, you've still got a
mission to fulfill.

The same thing applies to serving the Lord. If everybody decides to leave Jesus, you've got to go on with
Him. If someone falls by the wayside, you can't let it affect
your walk with Him. If an enemy asks if you believe in
Jesus, you say yes, even if it threatens your life.

Yes, there are hurts and pains in this life, but like the
soldier, you have a mission to fulfill. That mission is to
serve Jesus and to let your light so shine before men that
they may see your good works and glorify the Father, which
is in heaven (Matthew 5:16). Then you will be able to hear
Him say, **"Well done, good and faithful servant"** (Matthew 25:21).

Notes

Chapter 3, page 33

1. Webster's New Collegiate Dictionary (Springfield, Mass.: G. & C. Merriam Co., 1974)

Chapter 7, page 73

2. Jerry Savelle, *If Satan Can't Steal Your Joy ... He Can't Keep Your Goods* (Tulsa, Oklahoma: Harrison House, Inc., 1982)

3. Savelle

If you've gotten to this page, more than likely you have finished the book. Congratulations! Now that you've read it, let me encourage you to make a commitment to receive your relief from grief. For those of you who have taken a loss particularly hard, it means developing a stronger relationship with the Father God. If some part of this book has been helpful, review that part and write down at least three things that strongly ministered to you and put them into action immediately. Then write me at

James E. Price Ministries
P.O. Box 20129
Long Beach, Calif. 90801
E-mail: jeprice@aol.com
www.lbchristiancenter.org

About the Author

Pastor James E. Price founded James E. Price Ministries in 1983 and Long Beach Christian Center in 2002. From 1980 to December 2001, he was an assistant pastor at Crenshaw Christian Center, under the direction of his famous uncle, Dr. Frederick K.C. Price.

Pastor James, as many call him, was an undergraduate student at Pepperdine University in the early '70s when the school established a new campus in Malibu and put the old campus in South Central Los Angeles up for sale. With their beloved school facility on the market, he and a group of students prayed that a spirit-filled ministry would buy the 32-acre inner-city campus. Pastor James had no idea that exactly a decade later Crenshaw Christian Center, then one of the fastest growing churches in the nation, would be that ministry. When his uncle announced that the church had quietly purchased the property, "I almost fell out of my seat!" Pastor James said.

As a Vietnam-era veteran, Pastor James is well acquainted with the sorrows of loss, having seen several buddies fall on the battlefield and having been seriously and permanently injured in a mortar explosion. As assistant pastor at Crenshaw Christian Center and as a pastor on his own, he has performed hundreds of memorial services.

Pastor James and his wife, Dolly, have been married 33 years, and are the parents of three sons — James, Michael and Robert — and a daughter, Connie Marie. The couple lives in Carson, California.